TWELVE STEPS TO WHOLENESS

BY

STAN E. DEKOVEN, PH.D.

TWELVE STEPS TO WHOLENESS
COPYRIGHT © 1989 BY STAN E. DEKOVEN, PH.D.

ISBN: 1-884213-59-6

ALL RIGHTS IN THIS BOOK ARE RESERVED WORLDWIDE. NO PART OF THIS BOOK MAY BE REPRODUCED IN ANY MANNER WHATSOEVER WITHOUT THE WRITTEN PERMISSION OF THE AUTHOR EXCEPT BRIEF QUOTATIONS EMBODIED IN CRITICAL ARTICLES OR REVIEWS.

PUBLISHED BY:
VISION PUBLISHING
940 MONTECITO WAY
RAMONA, CA 92065
(760) 789-4700
WWW.VIU.COM

PRINTED IN THE UNITED STATES OF AMERICA

TABLE OF CONTENTS

INTRODUCTION 5
   How to Use This Book 5
   The Problem 9
   Rules Learned by Children in Shame-Based Families 10
   Grief Response 13
   Stages of Grief 13
   How Can I Be Sure I Need This Group? 22
   Becoming Stuck 22
   The Solution 25
THE GROUP PROCESS 27
   Guidelines 27
   Six Do's and Don'ts to Develop
   Your Own Support Group 32
   Group Suggestions for Leaders of Twelve Step Groups 33
   Rules for Group Discussion 34
THE TWELVE STEPS 37
   Step One 37
   Step Two 41
   Step Three 46
THE HEALING COMMUNITY 51
   Step Four 51
CHARACTER LIST 59
   Step Five 60
   Step Six 62

  Step Seven 65
  "The Several Objectives" of Steps Six and Seven Are: 68
  Step Eight 69
  Step Nine 72
THE COMPASSIONATE LIFE 75
  Step Ten 75
  Step Eleven 77
  Step Twelve 80
CONCLUSION 83

APPENDIX ONE: *Group Agreement* 85
APPENDIX TWO: *Sample Outreach Flyer* 87
APPENDIX THREE: *Sample Registration Form* 89

NOTES 91

THE TEACHING MINISTRY OF DR. STAN DEKOVEN 93

Introduction

Over the past many years, I have been conducting work shops and seminars across the country and internationally. The results have been most gratifying as believers begin to fully grasp God's overall plan for the healing and restoration of their lives. For many, the awareness of the Lord's great love, graciousness and power to transform lives, has had a liberating affect for which He deserves all the glory!

One of the needs expressed by many has been to have an ongoing group for those struggling to become whole in Christ. In praying about this need, I have chosen to adopt the *Twelve Step* model of Alcoholics Anonymous as a guide, with certain modifications, that beautifully corresponds to the three stages of our spiritual development as described in my book, *Journey To Wholeness: Restoration of the Soul.* [1]

This book is to be used in small group formats, as you will see in the "Group Process" section. It is my hope that many will find complete healing and wholeness regardless of the level of dysfunction of family raised in, for God can save us to the uttermost and transform even the chief of all sinners into the glorious image of His Son. This book can be used in various recovery formats to include grief and loss, adult children of alcoholics, etc.

How to Use This Book

This book is designed to be read and the outlines used in it, over and over again. There is really no special magic or unique key to resolving past conflict and achieving peace in the inner man. It is

---

[1] *Journey to Wholeness: Restoration of the Soul*, by Stan E. DeKoven, Ph.D. Vision Publishing, 1993.

a process that requires diligent hard work, discipline and patience to trust the Lord and the process. These characteristics are not normally part of one who was raised in a dysfunctional family. In fact, if you were able to easily discipline yourself to apply scripture to your life, you wouldn't need this book! So be aware, all of us using this program are fellow strugglers, *"Working out our own salvation with fear and trembling,"* (see Philippians 2:12).

Before beginning this, or any other *Twelve Step* study group process, it is important to ask yourself some important questions. Your answers will help you determine your readiness for the group process and very possibly your future success.

1. Can you commit yourself to the time involved?
   [ ] Yes   [ ] No

Ideally the group should be a high priority. I recommend that you develop and participate in a 13 to 25 week program, meeting weekly for 2 hours. This is in addition to your other church related obligations. Make sure that barring an emergency, you can complete your commitment to yourself, the group and the Lord. If you are unsure, seek counsel from your spiritual leadership, especially your pastor.

2. Do you really want to change?
   [ ] Yes   [ ] No

Many people will start a group hoping that their spouse will change, their circumstances will change, etc. We must accept the reality that the only person we can change is ourselves, with God's help and power. This group is designed for you to focus in on making changes in **your** life, transforming **your** mind, circumcising **your** heart. Be willing to trust the process. You did not develop physically overnight and you will not change emotionally and spiritually overnight. We must trust in the Lord to fully guide us. (See Proverbs 3:5-6).

3. Are you willing to submit to the process of change?
[ ] Yes   [ ] No

Jesus said that if you are to build a house, you must first *"count the cost..."* Growing in the Lord comes through discipline (see Hebrews 12), or teaching. This is not a painless process. As you go through the steps, you may feel worse before you feel better. This is expected. Again, you must be certain that you will complete the program before you begin. Once you have determined that you can and will make your best effort to allow the Lord to minister to you through the *Twelve Step* process, you are ready to take the next step.

4. Read

Most people find it helpful to read my books, *Journey To Wholeness: Restoration of the Soul*, or *Grief Relief* [2] for grief and loss recovery as a prerequisite to beginning the group. Further, listening to the teaching tapes based on these books can be of assistance in understanding the general plan that God has for us. It is recommended that you read beforehand, but if you cannot do so, the reading can be completed during the first three weeks of the group. You will find in *Journey To Wholeness: Restoration*

---

[2] *Grief Relief*, by Stan E. DeKoven, Ph.D. Vision Publishing, 1993.

of the Soul a typology of our physical/emotional development to maturity and our spiritual growth process. This gives you the "big picture" of God's marvelous plan. There is very little in this book that can be claimed as "new." It is a synthesis of the plan of God for our lives, presented in an understandable format. Neither this book, nor any other, is a substitute for the personal study of God's Word. Remember to read the Word of God daily along with doing your questions in this book, as you take your first steps toward transformation. *Grief Relief* was written for those who have suffered a significant loss. If you are in a grief process, the group and *Grief Relief* will help. It lists the specific stages of grief, the process of mourning and the hope that we have in Jesus Christ.

5. We have a head start.

It is important to remember that we have many things going for us as Christians, because of what Jesus has done for us through His atonement on the cross. These include:

a. When He ascended to be with His Father, *"He led captivity captive,"* (Ephesians 4:8). That is, all that binds, wounds, hurts, and destroys us was ultimately broken and eradicated for time and eternity on the cross of Calvary. All the guilt and shame, every dysfunctional thought and painful feeling was borne for us on the cross. We rely on the blood of Jesus, His power and sufficiency to continue to cleanse and restore us.

b. Jesus is now interceding (pleading our case and defending us) for us to His Father in heaven. *"He ever lives to make intercession for us as a great high priest,"* (Hebrews 7:25). What a wonderful thought to know that we have such a powerful advocate.

c. Jesus has given the Holy Spirit, Comforter (John 14 through 16), and Counselor to us. He comes along side of us, assisting us in our walk. He also reveals truth and will lovingly bring to the surface anything in our lives that needs transformation by God's great power. As we yield ourselves to Him, He will remove every stain, spot, or wrinkle from our lives, and prepare us to be His glorious bride (Ephesians 5:27). This is now happening throughout the Body of Christ and this guide is one of many tools to be used for this purpose.

d. Christ gave to the church the five-fold ministry to teach, train, exhort, rebuke, correct and encourage (Ephesians 4:11-12) His children to come to a place of completeness in Christ, conformed to His image. With all of these and the deposit of the gifts and grace in each of us, we can rest assured that in due time, we will become all God created us to be.

THE PROBLEM

Perhaps some of the following characteristics describe you as they do many adult children of dysfunctional families or those who have experienced a significant loss. I have outlined them for you here. Open your heart and mind to the Holy Spirit's work in your life, but remember, *"There is no condemnation to those in Christ Jesus,"* (Romans 8:1).

1. We become **isolated and afraid** of people and authority figures. **Angry people** and **personal criticism** frighten us. We either become dysfunctional ourselves or marry someone who is, or both. We find a compulsive personality, such as a workaholic, to fulfill our subconscious need for **abandonment**.

2. We view life as victims and we are attracted to weakness in our love, friendship and career relationships.

3. We have an overdeveloped sense of responsibility and it is easy for us to be concerned with others rather than ourselves. This helps us to avoid looking too closely at our own faults and to avoid responsibility for ourselves. Somehow we feel guilty if we stand up for ourselves instead of giving in to others.

4. We become addicted to excitement in all our affairs, we confuse love with pity and we tend to rescue others and try to "fix" them.

5. We have denied feelings from our traumatic childhood and have lost the ability to express even comfortable feelings such as joy or happiness.

6. We judge others harshly and fear the judgment of others; yet we also criticize and judge others.

7. We are terrified of abandonment and will do almost anything to hold onto a relationship rather than

experience the painful feeling of abandonment. We develop this from living in a compulsive environment where no one was emotionally "there" for us.

8. As all compulsions are a part of a family dysfunction, we took on symptoms early in childhood and carried them into adulthood. Even though we may never act out compulsive behavior ourselves, we have acquired unhealthy behavior patterns that have given us difficulty, especially in our intimate relationships.

This is a description, not an indictment. We have learned to survive by becoming reactors, rather than actors. We have learned that we can unlearn, however, as described in "The Solution."

Further, there are many rules we have learned in our dysfunctional family environment. These rules can bind us in our present life circumstances. Some of the rule are described here.

RULES LEARNED BY CHILDREN IN SHAME-BASED FAMILIES [3]

Each family has rules. There are rules about celebrating and socializing, rules about touching and sexuality; rules about sickness and proper health care; rules about vacations and vocations; rules about household maintenance and spending money. Perhaps the most important rules are about feelings, interpersonal communication and parenting.

Toxic shame (shame of oneself that poisons a persons thinking, feeling and behavior) is consciously transferred through shaming

---
[3] Taken from: *Healing the Shame that Binds You*, by John Bradshaw. Health Communication, Inc.

rules which are passed down through each generation. Some of these are:

Control: One must be in control of all feelings, interactions and personal behavior at all times.

Perfection: Always be right in everything you do (we learn to live according to an external image, an imposed measurement to which no one measure up).

Blame: Whenever things don't turn out as planned, blame yourself or others.

Denial of the Five Freedoms: Don't perceive, think, feel, desire, or imagine the ways you do; do these the way the perfectionist ideal demands.

The No-talk Rule: Don't speak of your loneliness and sense of self-rapture.

Don't Make Mistakes: Mistakes reveal the flawed, vulnerable self. To acknowledge a mistake is to open yourself to scrutiny. Cover up your own mistakes and if someone else makes one, shame them.

Unreliability: Don't expect reliability in relationships. Don't trust anyone and you will never be disappointed.

Grief Response

When a person suffers a significant loss, whether through divorce, death, or the loss of a friend or job, the reactions can be enormous. Although everyone responds differently to loss, based on past experience and individual differences, it is universally painful. There are certain stages of grief that have been identified by behavioral scientists and must be processed through for emotional, psychological and spiritual health and recovery. For the majority of men and women raised in dysfunctional families, a loss of the inner child or of childhood experiences occur, necessitating the development of denial and other defense mechanisms such as repression. When pain of loss, even loss in childhood is not resolved, a person can become "stuck" in their emotional growth. Therefore, a grief process is necessary for most people, whether due to adult losses or dysfunctional family life. To better understand the grief process the significant stages of grief are provided here. For more detailed information read, *Grief Relief.*

The Stages of Grief

Stage One: SHOCK

The first stage in grief is shock.

With shock, a kind of numbness envelopes you.

Shock is nature's natural insulation, cushioning the severity of the blow. Shock is a physical experience in which you might feel odd physical sensations, a "spaced-out" feeling, a tight knot in your stomach, or even the loss of your normal appetite.

You may notice that you become distressed over little things which normally would not mean that much to you, such as throwing a major tantrum when you discover a minor problem – perhaps it is the missing button on a favorite piece of clothing, or the failure of a child to take out the garbage – little things, made almost intolerable from the sudden shock of loss.

Or, you may not be able to remember small, common things such as your own phone number, or the name of a friend you see almost every day. These "memory blocks" are also a normal part of the shock stage.

Nervous laughter also occurs during this first stage of grief.

When I first heard that I had not been accepted into the college of my choice, my initial reaction was the inappropriate laughter of disbelief (a form of shock). I experienced shock in a similar way when my step-grandfather passed away. He was very special to me, and I didn't want to believe he was gone and strange as it might seem, an almost uncontrollable laughter was the result.

Shock and numbness will not prevent you from doing what you must do. You will act, at least in part, instinctively. Whatever your situation, you will normally retain the capacity to be rational. The numbness will soon wear away and real grieving will begin.

Even without these particular symptoms of shock, you still may cry out from your heart something like this: "Oh no, I can't believe he or she is gone!"

This too, is a form of shock.

In some cases, a person may act as if their loved one had not died for hours (normal) or even days (not so normal – if it continues, seek help), or they will act as though the loss had not occurred at all.

When you are hurting, you may appear not to care about others, but you are relying on automatic behavior, without thinking, because you are in a state of shock.

During this stage you may say, "I don't know what's happening to me," or, "Why can't I do something, why can't I think this through?" or even "Why don't I care about others?"

All of these reactions are normal for the first stage of grief – shock.

In time, the shock will wear off and you will once again come in contact with your real emotions.

STAGE TWO: DENIAL

Usually the stage after shock is denial.

Of course you understand intellectually what has happened through your loss, but on a deeper level, all of your habits and memories are denying the death or the loss that has occurred.

You may find yourself setting the wrong number of plates at the table, or saving bits of news for someone who will never be able to hear them again.

In one case, when a man lost his job, he kept working at home on a major business report for his previous employer that he "just had to finish," even though he was no longer employed. It was only after his wife loudly confronted him, claiming he had to stop the denial behavior, that he finally broke down and cried, sobbing, "Why me? Why me?"

Denial may surface in some form or another for many months or years. There is no set time schedule for moving through this stage.

Some deny death or loss by staying away from the grave or other reminders of their lost loved one. Others leave the deceased's room unchanged for a period of time. But, perhaps the most common type of denial is to just change the subject whenever circumstances about the pain or loss come up.

How many times, when you've questioned a friend or a relative about a shocking loss – such as a divorce – have you heard the answer, "I don't want to talk about it!?"

This is a normal denial, and will usually subside after the pain subsides.

Do what feels proper for you as you move toward acceptance. There simply are no absolute right or wrong time frames in these matters.

Please understand that keeping a few treasures and pictures in view indefinitely is not denial, but simply an affirmation and a reminder of the love you shared. A part of you will always grieve, but soon, you will be able to accept the death of the one you love through the love of Jesus Christ Who strengthens you.

STAGE THREE: FANTASY VS. REALITY

The third stage of your transition is a struggle between fantasy and reality (this can actually be seen as a component of denial).

You may find yourself experiencing some of these fairly typical reactions that I have had voiced from my clients:

"When I get up and go to the kitchen for breakfast, I almost expect my spouse to be there, waiting to greet me with a morning kiss."

"I caught myself looking around the backyard expecting to see my child out there playing. I even brought my child's bike in from the rain so it wouldn't rust."

"I heard someone pull into the driveway, and for a moment I thought my sweetheart was home from grocery shopping."

"I saw her walking in the supermarket, and from the back I was sure it was my wife. I found myself walking faster to catch up to her, only to remember my wife was dead."

Perhaps you find yourself doing, or wanting to do the things the two of you have always done, such as getting the mail, going for walks, or paying bills together. These are short fantasies and are a very normal way of wishing that things were different, wishing that your loved one was still with you.

Whether you only think of these fantasies or act them out, consider them as transitory – they will pass. They are healthy ways of experiencing grief relief and only reflect the cry in your heart that you "wish they had not gone."

To want everything to be the same in your life – just as it was before the loss or death – is very normal!

Most people in the grief process frequently move in and out of these experiences, from fantasy to reality to fantasy, with little or no control over such movement.

Although this is frustrating and confusing at times, please do not be alarmed by the behavior. It is a very normal part of the process.

Stage Four: **GRIEF RELEASE**

Sooner or later you will come to realize that your loss is real and the pain of this reality will penetrate to your deepest self. You will cry and weep – from deep within your gut. Your feelings will come pouring out like a fountain of sorrow.

You may even feel as though you are losing control of your feelings and emotions.

But do not let this worry you!

Since you first learned of your tremendous loss, you have come through many stages. These stages may have taken hours, days, or weeks, but you have come a long way! All the normal emotions that have been denied through these first stages now express themselves – it is a grief release.

Let it flow!

Let your emotions out!

This is one of God's ways of cleansing you from the pain.

After this grief release, much of your physical and emotional pain will fade away. Certainly the most noticeable and obvious signs of grief, such as shortness of breath, nausea, or choking sensations, will disappear.

Beware of those who try to comfort you by saying, "Don't cry, you'll be all right," or "Don't worry, God will take care of you."

These comments are well-intentioned, but are from misguided givers of advice (such as Job's friends).

Do not hold back on your crying.

Do not try to tell yourself you are a "bad Christian" because you are not rejoicing that your loved one is with God.

Do not allow the devil to condemn you for a "loss of faith" because you are hurting; and those around you are saying, "Trust God, trust God."

The grief you are experiencing is God's way of releasing your emotions and pain!

You need the time to cry and release your feelings!

Yes – God has promised to take care of you – and one way He does this is by allowing your grief to be eased through crying, by getting your feelings out so that you are free of them.

If you severely cut your arm and the pain caused you to cry, not one of these same people would say to you, "Trust God, trust God."

They'd tell you to cry – to let it out – because it hurts so much.

The same is true with grief. Emotional pain is no less real than the physical pain that comes with a cut arm!

You will always have the memories of the loss, but as with a scar from a wound long since healed, you will eventually no longer feel the sharp pain.

Do not reject those who try to give you false comfort – they are doing the only thing they know how to do to make you feel better. Just know that there is good health in releasing your feelings and easing your grief and that this process in no way indicates a lack of faith or lack of trust in God.

And, it is actually harmful to hold these emotions inside!

A grieving person who keeps his feelings inside and delays their release for an extended period may experience some strong negative reactions, even manifested in physical problems such as ulcers, severe headaches, and other stress-related illnesses.

STAGE FIVE: LIVING WITH THE MEMORIES

After you have experienced the therapeutic flood of grief from the previous stage, the pain of grief begins to ease. You are now emerging from the process to the victory of GRIEF RELIEF.

But, grief's slow work is not yet finished.

When you go to church for the first time without your mate, you may feel the sharp pain of grief because of his or her absence from the pew beside you.

If a parent who has lived with you has died, you may be reminded of your loss when you receive a Christmas card addressed to them.

When you drive by the building where you used to work before you were fired, pangs of anxiety and inadequacy might envelop you.

In ALL these instances, you feel the hurt or grief again.

Naturally, on the first anniversary of the death of your loved one, you will be reminded of them... and grieve. Naturally, when you meet an old work associate who reminds you of the job you used to have, you will grieve.

These experiences are very real and a completely normal part of the grief relief process.

Learning to live with memories is a long-term task.

You will meet people, go places and see thins that remind you of your significant loss. But in this stage, grief is not a constant painful process, but is aroused by specific incidents that trigger old memories.

STAGE SIX: ACCEPTANCE; AFFIRMATION

In this stage, you are now beginning to accept the loss and to affirm in your own life that you will go on living.

Good memories of the deceased are brought to your mind without stabbing pain and often with gratitude and pleasure for such recollections.

If you've just lost a major job, after a period of mourning, there comes a time when you say, "That's it! I've got to get on with my life."

When you are finally ready to decide to make a statement of acceptance ("I can't change it. It has happened, and it is over"), and a statement of affirmation ("It is time for me to start dating again") – then you are well on your way to a healthy, normal life!

I encourage you to entertain good memories.

Good memories will make it easier and easier to talk about your loved one and to appreciate your past relationship without wishing unrealistically that it could be restored.

You will start to show a renewed trust in yourself, as if to say, "I can make it." No matter how you express it, there is great hope when you begin to see good possibilities for yourself and your future.

Remember, often the process of grief relief takes years to fully complete.

There is no need to hurry it.

Grief moves at its own pace.

Trust the Holy Spirit, dedicate your grief process to the will of God and trust He will do a good work in you.

> *"Being confident of this very thing, that he who hath begun a good work in you will perform it until the day of Jesus Christ"* (Philippians 1:6).

During this stage of affirmation and acceptance, you will begin doing more things with others.

You may take your children to the beach and enjoy it. You may sponsor a wedding shower and not feel lonely for your ex-spouse.

You may go bowling with some of your ex-work associates without any strong pangs of remorse that you are no longer employed with their company.

You may reminisce about the good times you had with your spouse, and even laugh about some of the funny times, but without the hurt.

You are finding new meaning in what you do.

Celebrate the memories of your deceased loved one without being obsessed by these memories!

Celebrate the positive parts of your old job, your ex-spouse (in a divorce) without being obsessed by the negative factors in these events!

> *"O give thanks unto the LORD; for he is good; for his mercy endureth forever"* (I Chronicles 16:34).

As mentioned above, it is possible and often the case, that one can become stuck or partially fixated in a stage of grief or normal growth. When this occurs, many symptoms can develop which limit the range of experience of an individuals life. This limitation, or dis-ease, is what primarily leads one into treatment. All of us desperately desire freedom, a sense of purpose and to follow the plans of God for our lives. If we become "stuck" in our growth process, we must work through the barriers that develop, which is the purpose of the recovery/restoration process.

How Can I Be Sure I Need This Group?

Over the past few years, especially through research done with alcoholics and drug abusers, a fairly comprehensive profile of personality traits and behavioral repertoire has been discovered that, when in combination, indicate the probability of an individual being raised in a dysfunctional family. The following is a checklist of symptoms. If you answer yes to 50% of these, you could probably benefit from a *Twelve Step* program. I would encourage you to answer each question and discover for yourself the need (if you have one, if not rejoice and help others) in your life.

Becoming Stuck

For those in grief recovery, whether through being raised in a dysfunctional family or from significant loss, support is always helpful. If a person becomes unable to face their loss or process through to acceptance (in a reasonable time frame), a recovery group will be of significant benefit.

In the check list that follows, see if you identify yourself in several of the following traits. If you do, it's likely that you are co-dependent and are carrying your family dysfunction, or are stuck in the grief relief process.

- ☐ **Abandonment Issues** — You fear that people you care for will leave you.
- ☐ **Delusion and Denial** — You are not facing the truth in real life situations.
- ☐ **Undifferentiated ego mass** — You lack independent thinking, you can't express yourself.
- ☐ **Loneliness and Isolation** (Self-explanatory)
- ☐ **Thought disorders** — You see hallucinations (seeing things not there) and hear voices.
- ☐ **Control madness** — You compulsively try to control everything, fear when not.
- ☐ **Hypervigilant and high level anxiety** — Perfectionism.
- ☐ **Internalized shame** — Self-loathing, not because you did bad, but because you ARE bad!
- ☐ **Lack of boundaries** — You let others violate you. You are unable to keep from victimization.
- ☐ **Disabled will** — You are unable to make healthy decisions.
- ☐ **Reactive and reenacting** — You react to others and repeat the same old patterns.
- ☐ **Equifinality** — You are fatalistic, "What will be, will be."
- ☐ **Numbed out** — You have no sense of feeling at all.
- ☐ **Offender with or without offender status** — You have a sense of always wrong.

- ☐ **Fixated personality** — You are stuck acting in the same old way.
- ☐ **Dissociated responses** — There is a sense of you "not being here" when responding. You're out of touch.
- ☐ **Yearning** — Desire for parental warmth and approval.
- ☐ **Secrets** — Especially family secrets you can't tell.
- ☐ **Faulty communication style** — Placate, blame, project.
- ☐ **Underinvolved** — You withdraw from life.
- ☐ **Neglect of development dependency needs** — You don't nurture yourself. You have a poor self-image.
- ☐ **Compulsive/Addictive** — Same thing, without satisfaction.
- ☐ **Trance** — You carry the family spell.
- ☐ **Intimacy problems** — You can't get close or stay close to people.
- ☐ **Overinvolved** — You try to do everything to fill void.
- ☐ **Narcissistically deprived** — You never had anyone there just for you.
- ☐ **Abuse victim** — Physical, emotional, sexual.
- ☐ **Lack of coping skills** (underlearning) — You are unable to do certain things. You did not learn.
- ☐ **False self** (confused identity) — You try to be what others expect, but not real self.
- ☐ **Avoid depression** — You fill in with many activities.
- ☐ **Measured, judgmental and perfectionist** — You have to, should have, must, ought, can't inhibited trust, but can't believe others could or would care.
- ☐ **Loss of your own reality** — You are so involved in pleasing others, You can't care for yourself.

- ☐ **Inveterate dreamer** — You are so heavenly minded, you are no earthly good!
- ☐ **Emotional constraint** — You lack the ability to express your feelings.
- ☐ **Spiritual bankruptcy** — You can't relate to God and His work in your life.

Again, if you said "yes" to 50% or more of these items, you probably suffer from dis-ease rooted in childhood dysfunction or significant loss. However, do not despair. As Christians, we have a hope in God and by the power of the Holy Spirit and the assistance of skilled helpers in the Body of Christ. Healing and restoration is available.

THE SOLUTION

Though our parents gave us our physical existence, we now look to God, our Heavenly Father, as the initiator of our new life. We look to Him for direction to a new level of experience, a life of wholeness and healing of the past. We learn that we do not have to remain prisoners of our past.

Recovery begins when we learn about the problems of our family upbringing. We learn that it is three-fold: physical, spiritual and mental. We learn the three C's: we didn't cause it, we can't control it and we can't cure it. By educating ourselves about the problem, we begin a process that eventually leads us to forgiveness of our parents and the willingness to release them to God. We learn that real love cannot exist without the dimension of justice.

We learn to experience our feelings and then to express them. This builds self-esteem, which is a missing ingredient in our personalities. We learn that, in Christ, we are OK – we are not "crazy." With God's help and twelve steps based on scripture, we can recover from the effects of our traumatic loss or our negative family learning and turn our lives in a new and beautiful direction. As we learn to admit our powerlessness to change ourselves and other people, places and things, we let God begin to heal our thinking and our defects one day at a time. We learn to let God and the group nurture us and we learn to nurture and accept ourselves and others. This also works effectively with the losses in our life and we can overcome and renew our zest for living again.

As we begin to discover and love ourselves as God loves us, we will see beautiful changes in all our relationships – especially with our parents, ourselves and God. If we are married and if we have children, we will find healthier ways of interacting with these loved ones too. Finally, we become actors, rather than reactors. We will learn to risk new relationships without fear of rejection.

THE GROUP PROCESS

Small groups meeting together for a common purpose are not a new phenomena (in spite of what many humanistic psychologists would teach). In fact, our present popular Home Group or Fellowship boom is a variation on a New Testament model (see Acts 2). Small groups and group process is a powerful forum whereby God can move on our behalf.

In small groups, as in any gathering of people, there must be certain rules agreed upon by all of the adherents, strictly followed, if positive results are to occur. Without some clear understanding, any group can degenerate into a dysfunctional pseudo-family that will repeat the patterns that caused our initial problems. Therefore, it is important that each group member read and acknowledge the following rules and to the best of their ability, follow them. (A copy of these rules and a place for voluntary signature, is provided in the back of this book.)

GUIDELINES

1. **Confidentiality/Anonymity** – Each person in the group must have a sense that their basic boundaries will not be violated. One such guarantee of that is the pledge to allow all members of the group to have anonymity and confidentiality. All business transacted in the group is owned jointly by the group. As children raised in dysfunctional families, our right of privacy of even our thoughts and feelings was violated. It was not safe for us to share our feelings without reprisal.

To assure confidentiality, we ask you to keep everything you hear confidential in our meetings. No member of this group is ever to be discussed outside of this group, not even with another group member. We feel our healing is dependent upon the trust that we have in God and in one another and the freedom that we feel to share openly and honestly without fear of exposure outside of the meetings.

Therefore, <u>we agree to keep all communication and identities anonymous and confidential.</u>

2. **Freedom to express feelings without judgment** – As mentioned above, the freedom to express the full range of our emotions as children was controlled or criticized by our care givers. In the group, everyone must have the opportunity to express themselves without being put down. We do not need to be the Holy Spirit for others. In grief recovery, we need permission to express our feelings without condemnation.

   a. **Denial of Negative Emotions** – It is very important that each member of this group feel free to express negative emotions such as pain, grief, or anger. Much compulsive behavior is the result of not being in touch with one's feelings or being afraid to acknowledge or express these feelings. We should never cut another person off with a statement such as, "You're forgetting the Lord can bring good out of this," or "You have to have faith that this will work out." Such statements are true, but they are not helpful when used to cut a person off from expressing feelings. If anything, they create more distress by their implication that the person suffering is lacking in faith and is somehow not a good Christian. When our feelings are discounted, we feel invalidated. We stop sharing our feelings and we lose hope of working through and being freed from our pain.

<u>We will allow others to express their feelings without interruption, interpretation, or criticism</u>.

3. **Care-taking vs. Care-giving** – All of us have attempted to have our needs met by either plodding ahead without help (and blaming others for our failures), or by manipulating others to "help us" or "fix us." In the group, it is essential to resist the temptation to take the responsibility for the rescue of others, or to seek "guidance" from others in the group. If either strategy had worked before, we would not need the group process. Crosstalk is talking to another person about their problems rather than discussing your own problems. It is alright to refer briefly to what another person has said, but each of us needs to talk about our own experiences, feelings, and problems. For instance, "I felt scared when you talked about your relapse, because last week I had my own relapse (or problem)." We must be especially careful to avoid crosstalk which involves criticism, advice, or denial of another person's pain.

   a. **Criticism** – If we feel criticized or judged, our response will be to stop sharing and we will experience increased guilt, hopelessness and isolation. We need to be free to admit personal negative things, knowing that the response of the group will be loving acceptance. The only exception to the no criticism rule is when a member says or does something which violates the guidelines of this group. Such behavior is subject to discussion and group decision.

    b. **Advice** – We tend to resist advice, often because it leaves us feeling talked down to. Sometimes we feel the advice is given without understanding or sympathy for the particulars of our personality, our history, or our situation. Even when we know the advice to be good, we may feel powerless to follow it. As a result, even good advice may leave us feeling hopeless. We are able to learn and grow from receiving love, support and acceptance and from seeking others getting well through the twelve steps. What we share here is not advice, but our own experience, strength and hope.

    <u>We will resist care-taking or seeking to be taken care of by group members.</u>

4. **Honesty with kindness** (speaking the truth in love) – As we express our feelings, it is important to be as honest as possible with ourselves and others. Where dishonesty is perceived in the group, confrontation may be necessary, but only after the person has been heard and acknowledged. Even someone in self-deception has his/her own right to the self-deceit.

    <u>We will attempt to be open and honest, sneaking the truth as we know it in love.</u>

5. **Self examination vs. blaming** – Our goal is for our character to be transformed by the renewing of our minds (see Romans 12:1-2). We must look at ourselves, not blaming others or projecting anger. This is not the

same as placing responsibility for acts committed against us.

<u>We must own responsibility for our own problems, not blaming others.</u>

6. **Trust the process** – Each meeting is designed, step by step, to set the stage for the healing power of God to touch and transform us. Each step we take is a move towards our healing and restoration.

    <u>We will trust each other and the group process to the best of our ability.</u>

7. **Mutual accountability** – The last thing the Lord has given to us for our growth is the church, the Body of Christ. Through the body, we can gain the sense of family and intimacy we missed in our family of origin. Therefore we must be accountable to one another.

WE CAN DO SO BY:

a. Praying for each other daily.
b. Being available in crisis.
c. Loving enough to care and confront.
d. Enjoying fellowship in a local church.

<u>We will be mutually accountable to one another.</u>

SIX DO'S AND DON'TS TO DEVELOP YOUR OWN SUPPORT SYSTEM [4]

DO...

- Look for different qualities different people.

- Accept and enjoy what people have to offer.

- Accept the limitations of others.

- Offer only what you are willing to give.

- Realize your time and friendship are precious.

- Keep trying.

DON'T...

- Expect any one person to answer all your needs in friendship.

- Expect people to give what they cannot or will not give.

- Expect others to respond exactly as you would.

- Try to give them to everyone.

- Give up if you don't succeed immediately.

---

[4] From: Sternberg, *Be My Friend*.

GROUP SUGGESTION FOR LEADERS OF *TWELVE STEP* GROUPS

You will want to adhere closely to the suggestions listed here in establishing and running your group. Doing so will enhance your success and effective ministry to others.

1. If you are running your group under church sponsorship (which is my suggestion), you will want to be sure of pastoral support. You may have to spend some time justifying the need to a skeptical (justifiably so) pastor. Let the pastor review the materials and answer any question he/she may have. Most pastors want to see growth occur in their sheep and as long as you don't threaten him/her, their acceptance is fairly easy to obtain. Without their support, your group will have tough sledding, at best.

2. Allow at least four weeks between the initial announcement of the group and its actual beginning. This gives ample opportunity for recruitment, the purchase of books and supplies, etc. Once you get started, you don't want to have to stop because of logistical problems. To assist you, a Group Agreement, Sample Outreach Flyer and Sample Registration Form are available in Appendix 1-3.

3. Make sure you arrange for a room conducive for open discussion. A Sunday School room can be used, but a conference room with comfortable chairs is much preferred. Insure that it has adequate heating and air conditioning and a place for coffee and accessible restrooms.

4. The group should be arranged in a circle, with clear visibility for each member to see the others. Make sure there are no posts to hide behind.

5. Group size may vary, but I have found a minimum of six, and a maximum of sixteen to be best. If you have more, it is better to run a second group. Since it is not necessary to be a trained professional group facilitator (though some group experience is definitely helpful), multiple groups are quite possible.

6. Your starting time should be the same each week, with a closing time fifteen minutes after the start and a completion time of 1 1/2 to 2 hours. This helps build commitment from the group, as well as predictability and consistency – desperate needs of all adults from dysfunctional families.

Rules for Group Discussion

1. While others are talking, please let them finish without interruption.

2. No "fixing." We are to listen, support and be supported by one another – not give advice.

3. It's OK to feel angry here and to express your anger in the group. We will hear you, but try to be considerate of others in the room.

4. Speak in the "I" mode about how something or someone made you feel. Example: "I felt sad when..."

5. Keep sharing for no longer than five minutes, in order that others in the group will also be able to share.

6. Try to share from the heart as honestly as you can. It's OK to cry, laugh, and be angry in the group without condemnation from others.

7. Remember that some people are here for the first time – others for the 60th time. Group members are in various stages of recovery. Give newcomers permission to be new, and old-timers permission to be further along in their recovery. We are here to welcome everyone into our family and to help them feel safe about sharing their lives.

The Twelve Steps

Step One

"**We admit we were powerless over alcohol/drug abuse and compulsive behavior – (or reaction to our loss) and that our lives had become unmanageable.**"

God's Word says in Romans 7:15, *"For that which I do I allow not: for what I would, that do I not; but what I hate, that do I."*

When we think about our behavior as being unmanageable, it can be understood as a gross understatement. Most of us have had tremendous struggles because of our dysfunctional families or significant losses. As mentioned earlier in this book, most of us suffer from various symptoms that make our lives difficult, at best. The most important step that we can go through in becoming full, complete and whole as God would have us become, is to fully admit that we do not have any power within ourselves to overcome that which has beset us. In Hebrews chapter 12, verses 1-2, it talks about laying aside encumbrances and the weights and sins that do so easily beset us. In order to do that we must be willing to admit, "In and of myself I cannot accomplish the task." We must admit our powerlessness and acknowledge the unmanageability of our lives. We have now listed a few questions that would be helpful for you to answer for yourself and be ready and willing to share with your group on the second night of the *Twelve Step* program.

1. What makes me think my life has become unmanageable?

Describe, in detail, those areas of your life that seem to be beyond your control to change.

2. What things have I tried in the past to overcome my problem?

_____
_____
_____
_____
_____
_____
_____
_____
_____

Have they worked? If not, why not?

_____
_____
_____
_____
_____
_____
_____
_____
_____

3. What resources have I tried, if any, or people have I talked to trying to resolve the problems in my life?

___

4. Who have I depended upon and tried to manipulate or control in order to meet my needs?

___

It is vitally important that we acknowledge that without the power of the Lord Jesus Christ flowing within our lives, we cannot change. We know that Jesus is a change agent. He came to destroy the works of the devil and to heal all who were oppressed of the devil. Therefore we have a great hope. Although we cannot solve our problems ourselves, they can be solved when we admit our powerlessness and come to a place where we can turn our lives over to the Lord Jesus Christ.

"WE ADMIT WE WERE POWERLESS OVER ALCOHOL/DRUG ABUSE AND COMPULSIVE BEHAVIOR – OR SIGNIFICANT LOSS AND THAT OUR LIVES HAD BECOME UNMANAGEABLE."

God's Word says in Romans 7:15, *"For that which I do I allow not for what I would that do I not; but what I hate, that do I."*

Step Two

"WE CAME TO ACCEPT JESUS CHRIST AS OUR HIGHER POWER – BELIEVING HE COULD AND WOULD RESTORE US TO WHOLENESS."

Jesus said in Matthew 19:26, *"With men this is impossible; but with God all things are possible."*

This scripture certainly speaks to the condition of most people who suffer great loss or are raised in a dysfunctional family system. How we have tried to resolve the problems in our lives! How we have tried to restore our own lives to wholeness! Yet, the truth of the matter is, it is only through the transformational power of the Lord Jesus Christ that true change will ever occur. It takes great faith to believe that we will ever become full and whole in God. Part of the transformation process covered in the books suggested is a belief that we are new creations in Christ at the moment we come to know Jesus. This step helps to reconfirm that we are, through the power of God, becoming greater than we ever thought we could. We have found a power greater than ourselves that can restore us. That power is the Lord Jesus Christ.

Let's now ask some questions. Write the answers for yourself as honestly as you can. Be willing and ready to share with your group.

1. When did I come to know Christ as my Savior?

_____
_____
_____
_____
_____
_____
_____
_____
_____

Describe the circumstances, the setting and the initial experience.

_____
_____
_____
_____
_____
_____
_____

2. What happened at the time that you came to know Christ? Describe it.

3. How long was it before you recognized that the initial experience did not seem to last, that the underlying problems were still there?

4. How have you tried to resolve this conflict within yourself? Do you believe that you just need more faith?

5. If Jesus really can restore us, why is it that it doesn't seem as though He has?

What must we do to become fully whole in Him?

_____
_____
_____
_____
_____
_____
_____
_____
_____
_____

This is a hard one, in that those of us who accepted Jesus Christ as our Lord and Savior have made an initial commitment to Him. The Bible indicates that, at the moment we come to know Christ, something truly miraculous happens. There is a new birth and a new creation occurs; yet, the old nature, which Paul talked about as "the sin that is within me," still tends to control our lives. This is why we must continue with the process of *"working out our salvation with fear and trembling,"* and moving toward a place of wholeness in God. Our recovery takes time; it takes energy; it takes faith and an understanding of God's Word and His will for our lives. *"Do not be weary in well doing, for in due season you will reap reward if you faint not."* Keep believing that Jesus is restoring, do not give up. God really is on the throne and as you surrender more and more of yourself to Him, you will find that He will be able to change even the most despicable parts of your character.

"WE CAME TO ACCEPT JESUS CHRIST AS OUR HIGHER POWER – BELIEVING HE COULD AND WOULD RESTORE US TO WHOLENESS."

Jesus said in Matthew 19:26, *"With men this is impossible; but with God all things are possible."*

STEP THREE

"WE MADE THE DECISION TO TURN OUR WILL AND OUR LIFE OVER TO JESUS CHRIST."

Jesus said in Matthew 11:28-30, *"Come unto me, all ye that labor and are heavy laden, and I will give you rest. Take my yoke upon you, and learn of me; for I am meek and lowly in heart: and ye shall find rest unto your souls. For my yoke is easy, and my burden is light."*

Now we are coming to the crux of the matter. In reality, although we are born-again and Spirit-filled, there is still a part of us (usually our will, but sometimes our mind and emotions as well), that has yet to come under the Lordship of Christ. We must decide to fully turn our will and our life over to Jesus Christ. That is not a decision that can be made from the emotions, although many emotional appeals will bring you to the altar to do so. This is a decision that must be made from the will. Herein lies the major problem for most of us. Because of our loss of family we were raise in, our will has become disabled. The ability to feel, to think, to trust, to decide, has become disabled over time. Our lack of faith and confidence in ourselves leads to a lack of faith and confidence in the Lord. The inadequacies, inconsistencies, and instabilities of our family make it very difficult for us to make decisions and stick to them. If any of us could just "decide," wouldn't we have done it a long time before now? The surrender of our will and our lives to God takes a decision. We must have honesty, faith, and much prayer. As we do this, God by His Spirit will begin to transform us by the renewing of our minds. Don't miss this. Step three offers no compromise with reservation or delay. It calls for decision here and now. We are to surrender every part of ourselves to the Lord Jesus Christ for only He can truly restore us. We must recognize that we will ourselves to the Lord by faith. The important thing is not having a sense of that will power, it is being willing to practice it. We may not have all the understanding that we need, but what matters in the willingness to give our lives over. Jesus will hear our prayers. He will answer and He will help us as we are willing to turn our lives over to Him.

1. Write down different ways and times that you have tried to surrender your will to the Lord.

___

What has been the effect?

___

2. How long does that decision, usually emotionally based, last?

3. If you were to give your life totally over to the Lord Jesus Christ, what do you think would change?

How do you feel about that? Be willing to share your feelings with the group as openly and vulnerably as you can.

_____
_____
_____
_____
_____
_____
_____
_____

4. Are you now willing to give your life over to the Lord Jesus Christ?

_____
_____
_____
_____
_____
_____
_____
_____

If you are, be willing to do so both privately and with someone you can trust as you covenant together to become more and more what God wants you to be.

Recognize that this is a decision that leads to many other decisions. With each decision that we make to surrender our will to the Lord Jesus Christ, we give a little bit of ourselves, but not the totality. We can only give what we know of ourselves. As we grow in God, more and more of our self, of our old nature, of our faults and failures, are revealed by the Holy Spirit. That is part of the job or responsibility of the Holy Spirit. You must be willing to surrender your life to the Lord and preferably to do so by, *"Confessing your faults one to another, praying for one another that you may be healed. The fervent, effective prayer of a righteous man avails much,"* (James 5:16).

"WE MADE THE DECISION TO TURN OUR WILL AND OUR LIFE OVER TO JESUS CHRIST."

Jesus said in Matthew 11:28-30, *"Come unto me, all ye that labor and are heavy laden, and I will give you rest. Take my yoke upon you, and learn of me; for I am meek and lowly in heart: and ye shall find rest unto your souls. For my yoke is easy, and my burden is light."*

THE HEALING COMMUNITY

Steps four through nine deal with the aspect of the book *Journey to Wholeness* called the healing community. This book discusses a process that we need to go through in the Body of Christ to insure that we become whole in God. This process is not an easy one. It is one that is clearly delineated in the Word and has been rediscovered by human behavioral specialists. It is most powerful in bringing about the transformation of our very characters. I encourage you to go through this with a sense of faith and awe because God will do something miraculous as you remain in the group and become honest with yourself and others. Further, for grief recovery, we must be willing to look at our lives before our loss; as well as after and allow the Lord to heal our inner most wounds.

STEP FOUR

"WE MADE A FEARLESS MORAL INVENTORY OF OUR HEART AND SOUL TO BETTER UNDERSTAND OURSELVES."

God's Word says in I John 1:8, *"If we say that we have no sin, we deceive ourselves, and the truth is not in us."*

For most people the fourth step is by far the most problematic. It is problematic in that you are asking the Holy Spirit to reveal the intentions and motivations of your heart. Jeremiah 17:9 says, *"The heart is deceitful and wicked above all things. Who can know it?"* Verse 10 says that the Lord knows the heart. He understands the intentions of the heart. Further, Hebrews 4:12 says that the Word of God searches out the motivations and intentions of the heart. What we are working toward here is not just a change in behavior, but an internal change of our personality. This includes the surrender of self-centeredness; learning to practice honesty and humility, appreciation, forgiveness; promptness in forgiving wrongs and making amends; service to others; an example of a happy, positive life. All of us desire to have that and a step to doing that is to look honestly at the harmful characteristics of our own heart.

I do not believe that this needs to be done in an attempt to assassinate or condemn one's self. Romans 8:1 says, *"There is therefore now no condemnation to them that are in Christ."* That includes self-condemnation, at which most of us are very good. There is no need to condemn yourself. You must look clearly at your own life and determine what areas need to change. In order to do this effectively, you must be willing to allow the Word of God to tell you what are the "rights" and what are the "wrongs'" of your character. Much of the way to do this would be to read certain passages of scripture that deal with how we are to live before our fellow man. I would encourage you to read Matthew chapters 5 through 7, known as the Sermon on the Mount or the Beatitudes, and Galatians 5 which talks about the deeds of the flesh and the fruit of the Spirit. As you read these sections, be willing to write down and discuss in detail how you manifest certain characteristics in your everyday life. A very simple way to do this is to make a list of certain characteristics that must be worked on.

1. Do you have, as a part of your life, resentments that need to be changed?
   [ ] Yes   [ ] No

List those people that you hold resentment against.

_____
_____
_____
_____
_____
_____
_____
_____
_____
_____

2. Have you ever been, or are you now, dishonest in relationships with yourself and others? Write it down. Be honest.

_____
_____
_____
_____
_____
_____
_____
_____
_____
_____

3. How have you allowed self pity to keep you in bondage and from seeking relationships and restoration in your life?

___

4. How have you allowed jealousy to creep into your life?

___

How has it manifested in relationships with others?

5. Do you ever allow yourself to become critical or intolerant of others?

If so, how do you do that?

6. Do you allow fear to rule your life?

List your main fears.

_____
_____
_____
_____
_____
_____
_____
_____
_____

7. Do you have anger toward others?

_____
_____
_____
_____
_____
_____
_____
_____
_____

How do you express it?

What have you tried to do to control it?

Character List

List in the spaces below, the character flaws that you will bring to the Lord, with faith to believe that the Lord will remove those flaws. In each case, write the flaw, how you feel about it, the underlying false belief or attitude you have about yourself because of the flaw and the truth according to God's Word.

1. Flaw: _____

   Feeling: _____

   Belief: _____

   Truth: _____

2. Flaw: _____

   Feeling: _____

   Belief: _____

   Truth: _____

It is important to remember that none of us have perfect vision in our own lives. The reality is that we have blind spots. We are unable to fully look at all of our flaws. This is a defense mechanism that protects us from even greater harm. As you are doing your inventory of your life, you should not dig and probe trying to find every "jot and tittle" of problems. Bring this to the Lord asking the Holy Spirit to reveal any issues of false pride, resentment, jealousy, dishonesty, suspicion, criticism, intolerance, vindictiveness, self-centeredness, etc., so that you can be prepared to do something with those characteristics.

"WE MADE A FEARLESS MORAL INVENTORY OF OUR HEART AND SOUL, TO BETTER UNDERSTAND OURSELVES."

God's Word says in I John 1:8, *"If we say that we have no sin, we deceive ourselves, and the truth is not in us."*

STEP FIVE

"WE CONFESSED TO GOD, TO OURSELVES AND TO ANOTHER HUMAN BEING THE EXACT NATURE OF OUR WRONGS (SINS)." (THIS INCLUDES OUR REACTION TO OUR LOSSES).

God's Word says in James 5:16, *"Confess your faults one to another, and pray one for another, that ye may be healed. The effectual fervent prayer of a righteous man availeth much."*

It has been said that confession is good for the soul and is a primary part of the healing community. All of us must go through this process no matter how functional or dysfunctional our families may have been, or how great our loss. It is the beginning of repentance in our lives. Here is where you want to confess, which means to tell, your moral inventory to God and to at least one other human being. That one other human being can be a clergy member, pastor, counselor, sponsor, or someone else within your group. This is a very difficult thing to do, but it is tremendously cleansing. God promises healing as we confess and as we pray. Confession alone brings a certain amount of relief, but not total resolution. It takes prayer and believing God. The prayer of a person who knows Jesus and is walking in a right relationship with Him, avails much.

In this section, I want you to ask yourself the following questions:

1. Have I confessed all of my known sins, faults and negative characteristics to the Lord?

_____
_____
_____
_____
_____

How do I feel about this?

_____
_____
_____
_____

2. Have I confessed to at least one other human being?

_____
_____
_____
_____
_____

If not, when will I do so? DATE: _____/_____/_____

I cannot reiterate how important this step is and yet, how difficult it is for most people to do. Many people who work *Twelve Step* programs come to this place and never finish. This is very unfortunate. Once you have gone through this, you will realize how easy it really was. The Lord Jesus Christ and those who listen to your moral inventory are ready to accept you just the way you are. God is a loving God. He is a gracious and good God. He is more than ready to forgive and forget all sin; to bury them in the sea of forgetfulness. Part of the next steps will be to assist you in forgiving yourself and those who have hurt you.

"WE CONFESSED TO GOD, TO OURSELVES AND TO ANOTHER HUMAN BEING THE EXACT NATURE OF OUR WRONGS (SINS)." (THIS INCLUDES OUR REACTION TO OUR LOSSES).

> God's Word says in James 5:16, *"Confess your faults one to another, and pray one for another, that ye may be healed. The effectual fervent prayer of a righteous man availeth much."*

STEP SIX

"WE BECAME ENTIRELY WILLING TO CHANGE AND ASKED GOD TO FORGIVE AND DELIVER US FROM OUR SINS."

> Jesus said in Acts 3:19, *"Repent ye therefore, and be converted, that your sins may be blotted out, when the times of refreshing shall come from the presence of the Lord."*

This step is very important, in that, most of us are willing to lay our burdens down at the altar before the Lord, but we scoop them back up, put them on our backs and walk away from the altar with them. We must recognize that when God forgives, He forgets. We must learn that God will remove all of our character defects in His timing. We have been forgiven and delivered. The blood of Jesus Christ cleanses from all sin – past, present, and future.

1. Have I allowed God to forgive me and deliver me from my sins?

_____
_____
_____
_____
_____
_____
_____
_____
_____

2. In the past, how have I picked up my burdens and carried them with me?

_____
_____
_____
_____
_____
_____
_____

3. Am I willing to now leave them with the Lord?

If so, what are my strategies for doing so?

4. How would I be different if I really believed I was forgiven?

Here is the beginning of a very humbling part of your twelve steps. We must be willing to accept the fact that we have a loving God who will receive us just the way we are. One of the things that we desperately needed as children growing up in dysfunctional families, was a sense of love and acceptance. Here, God is offering this to us, and the group is offering it as well. We must be willing to allow ourselves to be forgiven for our short comings. None of us are perfect. *"None are righteous, no not one."* All of us deserve God's punishment and yet, He offers mercy. What a marvelous God we serve! Allow God to do the work of forgiveness and to deliver you. I would make the serenity prayer my prayer everyday, *"God, grant me the serenity to change the things I can, accept the thins I can't, and the wisdom to know the difference."* It is important to realize that, one day at a time, God is changing us. Every day and in every way I am getting better and better by the grace of Almighty God.

"WE BECAME ENTIRELY WILLING TO CHANGE AND ASKED GOD TO FORGIVE AND DELIVER US FROM OUR SINS."

Jesus said in Acts 3:19, *"Repent ye therefore, and be converted, that your sins may be blotted out, when the times of refreshing shall come from the presence of the Lord."*

STEP SEVEN

"WE HUMBLY ASKED GOD, IN THE NAME OF JESUS, TO REMOVE OUR FAULTS."

God's Word says in James 4:6, *"God resisteth the proud, but giveth grace unto the humble."*

After we have completed step five, humility has been experienced and self respect has been restored as a result of our admitting to God and to another human being the exact nature of our wrongs. Now we are suitably ready to carry through the provisions of steps six and seven. This brings us face to face with our real selves – the root of who we really are. In Isaiah, Jesus was described as a *"root out of dry ground."* Most of us can relate to that. We have no real source or substance as human beings. Truly, in and of ourselves we do not. Through the power of God's transformation, He can give us peace, restore our sanity and make us whole and complete in Him. In order to do this, we must humbly ask God in the name of Jesus, to remove our faults. Why would God want to do that for us? Have you ever asked yourself that question? Let's ask ourselves right now.

1. Why would God want to remove my faults from me?

_____
_____
_____
_____
_____
_____
_____
_____
_____

2. Can God do it?

3. Answer honestly before yourself. Are you willing to allow God to remove your faults?

Are you willing to cooperate with God?

I would like to read several objectives of steps six and seven which come from *The Little Red Book* which talks about the *Twelve Step* program.

"The Several Objectives" of Steps Six and Seven Are:

1. To become honest and humble. To willingly seek God's help without reservation.

2. To perfect ourselves in the practice of unselfish prayer.

3. To be aware of our defective character traits.

4. To desire their removal.

5. To surrender completely all defects of character.

6. To believe that God can remove them.

7. To ask Him to take them all away.

I believe with all of my heart, that if you will submit to this process and ask God, you will receive. That asking, as recorded in the book of Matthew is, "keep on asking, keep on seeking, and keep on knocking." We ask God for help. We thank Him for recovery. We maintain our determination to grow in the things of God. There is nothing outstanding about the way you pray. It is the act of obedience and humility asking God to change you. He will give to you fully the fruit of the Holy Spirit. He will teach you to be cooperative, honest, tolerant, forgiving, faithful and to have honest, unselfish love toward others.

> "WE HUMBLY ASKED GOD, IN THE NAME OF JESUS, TO REMOVE OUR FAULTS."

God's Word says in James 4:6, *"God resisteth the proud, but giveth grace unto the humble."*

STEP EIGHT

> "WE MADE A LIST OF ALL PERSONS WE HAD WRONGED AND BECAME WILLING TO MAKE AMENDS TO THEM ALL."

Jesus said in Mark 11:25, *"And when ye stand praying, forgive, if ye have ought against any: that your Father also which is in Heaven may forgive you your trespasses."*

Here is a way of practicing and/or working through our problems from our past. We must recognize that mistakes that we have made, sins that we have committed toward others, need to be corrected. We cannot always actually make amends for wrongs that we have done. We must be willing to do so as long as it will not cause greater harm to the person with whom we need to make amends.

1. Am I willing to make amends to people that I have wronged?

_____
_____
_____
_____
_____

2. Make a list of all persons that you have wronged. The types of people that you might list includes:

_____
_____
_____
_____

   a. Friends who you may have hurt verbally, non-verbally, or by not doing things promised.

   b. Family members that you have hurt in the past.

   c. Creditors.

   d. The deceased – with this group we must bring our amends to the Lord and receive His forgiveness for the things that we have done wrong.

_____
_____
_____
_____
_____
_____
_____

Place a number one (1) beside each name of those who are alive and available to be talked to about the wrongs that have been done. Place a number two (2) beside each name of those who are not available and/or it would cause greater harm to share with them and make amends than it would to keep silent.

I would strongly encourage you to share openly with the group and seek wise counsel before making amends to any individual. This is a form of maturity that is necessary in the making amends process.

3. What hindrances do I have to making amends with others?

_____
_____
_____
_____
_____
_____
_____
_____
_____

It is very important that we make amends, make things right, in order to live in a right relationship with God. Once you have done so, there is no longer any fear of reprisal. That is a beautiful and exciting feeling — to be able to walk in a place where you can live and let live, knowing that there is little or no hurt feelings between you and another.

> "WE MADE A LIST OF ALL PERSONS WE HAD WRONGED AND BECAME WILLING TO MAKE AMENDS TO THEM ALL."

Jesus said in Mark 11:25, *"And when ye stand praying, forgive, if ye have ought against any: that your Father also which is in Heaven may forgive you your trespasses."*

STEP NINE

"WE MADE DIRECT AMENDS TO THOSE WE HAD WRONGED WHEREVER POSSIBLE, EXCEPT WHEN TO DO SO WOULD INJURE THEM OR OTHERS."

Jesus said in Matthew 5:9, *"Blessed are the peacemakers: for they shall be called the children of God."*

Our goal is to make peace with people without bringing further harm. An example of this could be where you have said or done something behind their back and they do not know about it. To go and tell them about it could cause more harm to them than good. Those things should be confessed to the Lord and perhaps, to your sponsor or discussed in the group. Forgiveness needs to be received.

1. Have I made amends to those that I have hurt?

2. Who should I not make amends to?

_____
_____
_____
_____
_____
_____
_____
_____
_____

Why not?

_____
_____
_____

3. What keeps me from following through on this important step?

_____
_____
_____
_____
_____
_____
_____
_____
_____

The Compassionate Life

Step ten begins the process of living out the compassionate life discussed in *Journey to Wholeness*. We will learn to live as fully and completely as possible the way Jesus did, lovingly reaching out to meet the needs of a lost and broken world. In terms of the grief process, we are moving towards acceptance of our loss and the re-embracing of life.

Step Ten

"We continue in the way of the Lord – repenting and asking for His forgiveness when we stumble."

God's Word said in I John 1:9, *"If we confess our sins, he is faithful and just to forgive us our sins, and to cleanse us from all unrighteousness."*

This is such a beautiful scripture. The reality of being human is that we all make mistakes. When we do, we must practice the process of putting off the old, renewing our mind and putting on the new. We must practice making things right with people. We must practice asking God for forgiveness and receiving that forgiveness without condemning ourselves. This is an ongoing lifestyle that must be developed.

1. Can you give an example where you have stumbled and have/have not been through the process of repenting during this past week?

_____
_____
_____
_____
_____
_____
_____
_____
_____

2. Is there someone that you are still harboring resentment, anger, or jealousy toward that you need to make things right with?

_____
_____
_____
_____
_____
_____
_____
_____
_____

If so, when will you do so? DATE: _____/_____/_____

Discuss your feelings openly with the group.

_____
_____
_____
_____
_____
_____
_____
_____
_____
_____

"WE CONTINUE IN THE WAY OF THE LORD – REPEATING AND ASKING FOR HIS FORGIVENESS WHEN WE STUMBLE."

God's Word said in I John 1:9, "*If we confess our sins, he is faithful and just to forgive us our sins, and to cleanse us from all unrighteousness.*"

STEP ELEVEN

"WE SEEK GOD'S WILL FOR OUR LIVES DAILY THROUGH PRAYER AND THE READING OF HIS WORD – PRAYING FOR THE POWER OF HIS HOLY SPIRIT IN ORDER TO WALK CLOSELY WITH HIM."

God's Word said in Philippians 4:6-7, "*Be careful for nothing; but in everything by prayer and supplication with thanksgiving let your requests be made known unto God.*

And the peace of God, which passeth all understanding, shall keep your hearts and minds through Christ Jesus."

Every individual believer must be willing to give away their own life. In order to do so, to live out a compassionate life, you must be strengthened daily by prayer and the reading of God's Word. It is amazing to note how many pastors do not spend private time continuing to develop that intimate relationship with the Lord Jesus Christ. This is the foundation for everything we do. It is not our relationship in the church; it is not our service for the Lord. He can live without that. What He wants is intimate fellowship with us. We must be willing to walk closely with Him by the leading of the Holy Spirit.

1. Have you developed a daily devotional life?
   [ ] Yes   [ ] No

   If not, why not?
   _____
   _____
   _____

2. What could you do to develop your devotional life?
   _____
   _____
   _____
   _____
   _____
   _____

3. Ask of the group how they function in this area. Covenant with one another to develop the intimate relationship by daily reading and prayer.

___

I cannot emphasize enough the importance of keeping your hearts and minds through Jesus Christ. The devil is constantly attacking us, especially those of us raised in dysfunctional families. Self pity is often the door through which he attacks the grieving. It is vital that we keep a close relationship with the Lord and with one another. It is important to be vulnerable with each other, to be willing to confess faults and to lay your life open before the Lord and others that you can trust.

"WE SEEK GOD'S WILL FOR OUR LIVES DAILY THROUGH PRAYER AND THE READING OF HIS WORD – PRAYING FOR THE POWER OF HIS HOLY SPIRIT IN ORDER TO WALK CLOSELY WITH HIM."

God's Word said in Philippians 4:6-7, *"Be careful for nothing; but in everything by prayer and supplication with thanksgiving let your requests be made known unto God.*

And the peace of God, which passeth all understanding, shall keep your hearts and minds through Christ Jesus."

STEP TWELVE

"WE HAVE BECOME NEW CREATURES IN CHRIST – FREE OF ABUSIVE AND COMPULSIVE BEHAVIOR, OVERCOMING OUR LOSSES – AND WE SEEK TO CARRY THE GOOD NEWS OF CHRIST AND THE PRINCIPLES OF RESTORATION TO OTHERS, AS WE CONTINUE TO LIVE BY THESE STEPS."

Jesus said in Mark 5:19, *"Go home to thy friends, and tell them how great things the Lord hath done for thee, and hath had compassion on thee."*

This is such an interesting statement. It is both a truth and a becoming truth. All of us are free. Jesus has made us free. And yet, we are becoming more free all the time as we continue through our *Twelve Step* process. As we continue in our relationship with the Lord, reading His Word, praying, worshipping, witnessing, we grow more in Him. There is a responsibility that we have to carry the good news of Christ, the power that He has to restore lives and to live that life before others. That is really our testimony. Revelation 11:10 says *"For they overcame him* (i.e. the devil) *by the blood of the Lamb and by the word of their testimony, and they loved not their lives unto death."* What a beautiful verse of scripture. All of us are truly more than conquerors in Christ Jesus. To live that conquering life we must daily submit our lives and admit our helplessness. We must daily confess our faults. We must daily read the Word. We must daily walk in the light of these twelve steps. As we do, God will continue to work out all of the garbage in our lives.

We will grow more and more faithful in Him. It is very, very important that we continue to live according to these steps and the principles outlines in the Word of God. As we do so, God will pour out His blessings upon us.

1. When was the last time I shared my faith in the Lord Jesus Christ?

_____
_____
_____
_____
_____
_____
_____
_____
_____

2. What keeps me from witnessing?

_____
_____
_____
_____
_____
_____
_____
_____
_____

3. What might I do to reach out to those in my community?

_____
_____
_____
_____
_____
_____
_____
_____
_____
_____

I am willing and I have made a strategy to reach out to someone in my world with the gospel of Jesus Christ. I trust that all of you will do that because I know that there is no greater relationship than the relationship that we can have with Jesus Christ and an honest relationship with one another as brothers and sisters in the Body of Christ.

"WE HAVE BECOME NEW CREATURES IN CHRIST – FREE OF ABUSIVE AND COMPULSIVE BEHAVIOR OVERCOMING OUR LOSSES – AND WE SEEK TO CARRY THE GOOD NEWS OF CHRIST AND THE PRINCIPLES OF RESTORATION TO OTHERS, AS WE CONTINUE TO LIVE BY THESE STEPS."

Jesus said in Mark 5:19, *"Go to thy friends, and tell them how great thins the Lord hath done for thee, and hath had compassion on thee."*

Conclusion

If you have just gone through this program, through all *Twelve Steps*, you have most likely solved many problem areas in your life. However, you will also recognize that you are not yet complete and whole, but that you are moving in that direction. As you continue to practice these things with the Lord and with others, you will find that you will grow daily in the ways of God. Once you have been through the process the first time, the majority of things that need to change has been done by the power of the Holy Spirit. We must choose to believe and receive His forgiveness, restoration, and healing and to practice those things that we have learned.

I trust that you will continue to grow and support your local church and be more involved in reaching out to those who hurt, living out the compassionate life style in accordance with the will of the Lord.

Appendix 1: Group Agreement

1. I agree to keep all communication and identities anonymous and confidential.

2. I will allow others to express their feelings without interruption, interpretation, or criticism.

3. I will resist care-taking or seeking to be taken care of by group members.

4. I will attempt to be open and honest, speaking the truth, as I know it, in love.

5. I will own responsibility for my own problems, not blaming others.

6. I will trust the members of the group and the group process, to the best of my ability.

7. I will be accountable to the members of the group; and, the other members of the group will be accountable to me and each other.

Signed: _____

Witness: _____

Date: _____

APPENDIX 2: SAMPLE OUTREACH FLYER

CHRISTIAN GROWTH GROUP
AT
FAMILY CARE CENTER
BEGINNING TUESDAY EVENING FROM 6:30 - 8:00 P.M.
WITH DR. STAN E. DEKOVEN

- Participants will learn and practice discipleship and healing for broken relationships and past hurts.
- Learn to listen to others and respond with compassion.
- Offer and receive support and assistance in a safe, confidential environment while building new relationships.
- Work through conflicts in a Christian fashion (Ephesians 4:25-5:2).
- Learn to grow towards maturity in Christ as we move through life's transitions.
- The purpose of the Family Care Center is to assist individuals, families and groups to become all that God has created them to be. It is only through Jesus that we can become whole and He uses members of the Body of believers, the Church, to help in that process.

For More Information Call:
Dr. Stan E. DeKoven
940 Montecito Way
Ramona, CA 92065
(760) 789-4700
A Program of Vision Christian Ministries

APPENDIX 3: SAMPLE REGISTRATION FORM

REGISTRATION FOR *TWELVE STEP* PROGRAM

Name: _____

Address: _____

City, State Zip _____

Type of Family Dysfunction:
- ☐ Alcohol
- ☐ Drugs
- ☐ Abuse
- ☐ Grief/Loss

Other: _____

Present Compulsion:
- ☐ Work
- ☐ Fear
- ☐ Eating
- ☐ Anger
- ☐ Sex
- ☐ Drugs

Other: _____

Notes:

The Teaching Ministry of Dr. Stan DeKoven

Dr. DeKoven conducts seminars based on his books in Practical Christian Living nationally and internationally. He is available for limited engagements for church seminars, retreats and conferences.

For a complete listing of topics and books, you can contact:

Dr. Stan DeKoven, President
Vision International University
Walk in Wisdom Seminars
940 Montecito Way
Ramona, CA 92065
(760) 789-4700
1-800-9VISION

Other Books by Dr. DeKoven on similar topics:

Grief Relief
Journey to Wholeness: Restoration of the Soul
40 Days to the Promise: A Way Through the Wilderness
Marriage and Family Life: A Christian Perspective
Turning Points: Ministry in Crisis
On Belay! Introduction to Christian Counseling
Family Violence: Patterns of Dysfunction
The Healing Community
Substance Abuse

To purchase, contact Vision Publishing at the above address.

www.ingramcontent.com/pod-product-compliance
Lightning Source LLC
Chambersburg PA
CBHW030002050426
42451CB00006B/87